THE REALITY OF SAVING

Faith

THE REALITY OF SAVING

Faith

One Man's Testimony of God's Saving Grace

JOSHUA M. SPAULDING

Foreword by

PASTOR ROB PELKEY

ETERNAL*Answers*
ETERNAL ANSWERS FOR A TEMPORARY WORLD

Eternal Answers Ministries
www.EternalAnswers.org

Contact the author personally:
contact@EternalAnswers.org
(812) 698-7659

The Reality of Saving Faith
by Joshua M. Spaulding
Foreword by Rob Pelkey

Copyright © 2024 by Joshua M. Spaulding

Printed in the United States of America

ISBN-13: 978-0692452257 (Eternal Answers Ministries)
ISBN-10: 0692452257

All Scripture quotations are from the King James (KJV) Bible.

Updated July 2024

Dedication

To souls.

Acknowledgements

To my wife, Claudia, and my two boys, Aaron, and Clayton. Thank you for your love, support, and forgiveness through the many times when I didn't deserve it.

I thank my mother for pointing me to Christ throughout my childhood and teenage years, even during those years of rebellion. Thank you, Mom, for your love and prayers. I love you!

I am eternally grateful for the mentorship, fellowship, and encouragement of Pastor Rob Pelkey. Your mentorship has been invaluable. I still had a great deal of "baggage" as a new believer, and you took me under your wing and guided me through a time when many others might have grown impatient with me. I am also so grateful for my pastor's wife, Joan, and son, Nathan.

I am also grateful for the fellowship and love of the members of Sherwood Hills Baptist Church in Indianapolis, Indiana. As a new believer, I was blessed to be a member of such a loving and encouraging group of Christians.

I also want to thank Pastor Michael Morrow for planting that gospel seed all those years ago. Thank you especially for your counsel when I needed it the most.

Table of Contents

Foreword

Joshua Spaulding came into our lives and our church about two years ago [2013]. What a blessing and a privilege to hear his "newborn" testimony and to watch him grow over the months. He is a faithful disciple of our Lord Jesus Christ.

I know his testimony and presentation of Gospel Truth, which is contained in this small volume, will be a source of great spiritual gain to all who read it and take it to heart. Believers will be thrilled as they read it. Those "lost" need to read this, whether they are "religious" and lost or "worldly" and lost.

What a testimony to the power of the Gospel and the amazing saving Grace of God!

Rob Pelkey
Pastor, Mt Zion Baptist Church
Sellersburg, Indiana

Introduction

Proverbs 14:12 *"There is a way which seemeth right unto a man, but the end thereof are the ways of death."*

For a majority of the first thirty years of my life, I was like the average American. I was a self-proclaimed Christian. Although I got into some trouble around the age of eighteen, I was what many would consider to be a good person. I didn't murder anyone. I didn't rape anyone. If someone fell, I would help the person up. I was usually kind to people. By the standards of the world, who are willing to forgive a few mistakes, I was good.

I had a very small spiritual appetite because I was filled up with the world. I saw devout Christians (as opposed to those like me at that time who were Christian in name only) as weak people who needed a crutch. I thought they must have depressing lives and clung to blind faith to provide hope to get through life.

I also saw hypocrites gossiping and talking unkindly about others, or doing other sinful things, while attending church every Sunday and/or calling themselves, "Christian." To me, aside from a small number, most of these people didn't seem any different from people of other beliefs. As a self-proclaimed Christian I was no better, but I didn't embrace Christianity. I didn't go to church, and I didn't claim to know any more about God than the next guy. So, to me, these churchgoers were far worse than I was.

Even the Christians who didn't appear to be obviously hypocritical, just seemed like "prudes" who thought they were better than everyone else. They only wanted to talk to you to strengthen their own faith and feel like they were pleasing God. To me there was no such thing as unquestionable truth, so anything they said to me was just an opinion.

I remember thinking that it was ridiculous to believe that the God of the universe will decide whether people go to paradise for eternity or burn in Hell for eternity, based solely on whether they believed that a Man existed and died on a cross. But I liked hearing things like "God is Love" and "God is forgiving" and "God has a wonderful plan for your life" so I gave intellectual ascent to Christ living, dying on the cross, and rising from the dead three days later.

Christianity was not real to me in my heart. I believed that what was said about Christ might be correct, but I had more of an agnostic viewpoint in my heart. I thought of the Bible as just a book that had probably changed over the years. I figured if God wanted to tell me something important, He would just appear to me and say the words. If that didn't happen, I imagined, then I couldn't possibly be held accountable for anything when I stood before Him.

My main purpose in life was to be happy. I believed the only way to be happy was to fulfill the desires of my heart. The primary desires of my heart were to fulfill my lusts in any way possible and to make as much money as possible.

This was my life before a series of events caused me to consider and seek after the meaning of life like never before. Then, on December 19, 2012, something happened that would change me *forever*.

This book is my story of how Christ saved my soul. My prayer is that Christ would be glorified in it as His love and mercy toward this sinner is told.

Whether you have a testimony of the rebirth (John 3:3), or you still need to be born again, I pray that this book will be a blessing to you and will bring Him glory!

Joshua M. Spaulding

- 1 -

Lessons from Iraq

"A general lack of humility"

In 2003 I was deployed to Iraq. I was part of an Army unit that was sent into Iraq at the very beginning of the war. We launched many missiles into Baghdad. Though we were causing much death, I knew they hated our Country, so I was content. My conscience was fine.

After the initial invasion ended, the Iraqi military was defeated, and we began our occupation of the country. My unit was involved in various missions after that. Most of these missions required traveling in convoys for many miles at a time. Although the Iraqis were generally nice to us and were more interested in getting American snacks and cigarettes than anything else, some hated us and didn't try to hide it.

I remember going into "Ambush Alley" in Nasiriyah (a city almost entirely filled with Shiite Muslims) within a few days of a battle that resulted in many fatalities and a few U.S. prisoners of war (including now famous Jessica Lynch). Just as we got there, our convoy stopped. There were hundreds of Iraqis all around us and these Iraqis, for the most part, weren't amused. We knew that a stationary convoy was like a sitting duck. Those were the most intense moments of my life.

Our convoy eventually started moving again and as far as I know we did not receive any enemy fire that day. That situation changed my perspective though. The intensity of those few hours made me realize I was no longer in the "safety bubble" of Germany, or the U.S... I knew that I couldn't judge the entire population by the positive attitude of the "snack seekers."

As our unit carried out various missions, we would go on long convoys. We all knew that getting cut off from the convoy in a heavily congested area could result in an ambush. So, if an Iraqi car (or anything for that matter) tried to cut into our convoy, we would force our way through by any means necessary. If we had to drive over a car with our HEMTT trucks (big ammunition trucks that we drove most often in our convoys) in order to stay within the convoy, then that's what we did.

Being intolerant of anything that tried to get into our convoy was necessary. What wasn't necessary was enjoying it, but I did. We enjoyed showing force and didn't care much about what the consequences might be.

I got out of the Army in 2007 as a sergeant, after five years. As I grew a little older and matured, I began to think about the Iraqis whose cars were damaged (among other things). I would think about the families they might have had. What if we tore up the car that a family with small children depended on to get food and other necessities? I also thought about their financial situations. Most were poor. Those cars were probably the most expensive things they owned.

At another time during my deployment to Iraq, I was on a special taskforce (we called ourselves "Tiger Team"). We were issued several armored SUV's. When we drove through a city, heads turned because you just didn't see nice SUV's every day in Iraq. People naturally assumed we were transporting VIP's.

One day, out of nowhere, about a hundred feet ahead of us in another lane, a large truck full of fruit flipped high into the air. The truck landed in a marketplace on the side of the road, hitting bystanders. I remember looking out and seeing the truck upside down. The heads of the two men in the truck were smashed. There were several other dead bodies and injured people lying around that had been hit by the truck. Most of the people nearby continued as if it was just another day. Several people rushed to the victims, not to help, but to loot the dead bodies.

I remember specifically, after we reached our destination of Taji, that most of the other soldiers on the team didn't seem to be very affected by it either, at least not outwardly. They just carried on, and we didn't even talk much about it. That really shocked me because I had never seen such a disregard for human life. Mainly the attitude of the Iraqi citizens at the scene shocked me, but also the response of my fellow soldiers. That isn't to say that they were all cold-hearted and didn't care. I know that wasn't the case. But in my heart, I was hurting and shocked. Many people had just lost their lives and I was expecting a different reaction.

How many kids had just lost their mom, dad, or both? How many parents just lost a child? How many people lost a sibling? How many families relied on one or more of the people who had just died?

Those questions ran through my head. I'll never forget that day — not only the accident and dead bodies, but the reaction of just about everyone else, both American and Iraqi.

Before this tragedy I was generally apathetic about things that didn't affect me directly, but afterwards I began to see my own wickedness, and that of others. I realized, for the first time in my life, that human life really wasn't very important to society in general.

- 2 -

An Unforgettable Meeting

"Jesus paid it all!"

Shortly after leaving the Army in 2007, and after briefly moving back to my hometown of Washington, Indiana, I moved my family into a small apartment in Evansville, Indiana. I had started an internet marketing business while I was still in the Army, and I was making enough money from that to pay the bills and put food on the table. I was passionate about making money online, and I was doing very well for the short amount of time that I had been active in it.

A few thousand people had signed up for my email newsletter to learn how to improve website rankings in search engines and increase traffic to their websites. One of those people was a pastor by the name of Michael Morrow, who lived just over the Indiana border in Kentucky. He was spreading the gospel online.

I didn't know Pastor Morrow at that time, but after he received an email that I sent out to my newsletter subscribers, he noticed that I had included my address. Since he didn't live far from Evansville, and he was planning to be in the area, he contacted me and asked if we could have coffee at a local bookstore to discuss internet marketing. I agreed to meet him.

The day came and oddly enough, though it was over seven years ago [2008], I still remember parking my car and walking into the bookstore. It's odd because this meeting, to be honest, wasn't important to me, as bad as that may sound. I didn't know him. I didn't know he was a pastor. I had other things to do, and I really didn't want any coffee. But since the bookstore was across the street and I had already agreed to meet him, I went ahead with the appointment.

When he arrived, we greeted one another. I answered a few questions that he had about internet marketing and explained some things that I was doing successfully with my websites. He seemed interested at first, but his interest in the topic seemed to gradually decline the more we talked.

After a few minutes he asked me, "Do you mind if we discuss the Scriptures for a few minutes?" I hesitated. I'm sure I was noticeably surprised at the question. Then I answered "Sure. My mother and grandmother are both real religious." What that had to do with anything I don't know.

He proceeded to tell the story of how the Lord Jesus Christ had convicted him of his sin many years earlier and how He saved him — how he was "born again."

He told me the gospel . . . God is sinless and holy, we are all sinful and unholy, and Jesus Christ, God in the flesh, came to live a perfect life without sin. He told me how Christ willingly died as our substitute, to satisfy God's righteousness on our behalf before rising from the dead three days later. He then told me that because of Christ's death, burial, and resurrection, I could be saved by grace, through faith.

When he got to the part where Jesus died for sinners, he said something that would stick with me forever. He said, "Jesus Christ paid it all." He explained that there was no more work that needed to be done. We are saved by grace through faith. That was a profound statement to me. I had always seen two kinds of people who professed Christianity:

1. Those who I considered to be hypocrites who said they were Christian but lived sinful lives.

2. Self-righteous people who didn't extend the same love and forgiveness to those outside their religious circles as Christ, who they claimed to know, supposedly did for them.

Many people from both groups would agree that all who don't believe in Jesus Christ would go to Hell. Yet no one *that I knew* from either group seemed very interested in the spiritual status of others.

If you see someone walking toward a cliff, whether you know them or not, you're going to do everything you can to persuade them to change course to avoid that cliff!

If the faith of these people was real, I knew they would want to make sure I wasn't headed toward Hell, not just out of their obligation to obey Christ and spread the gospel, but because I was headed toward something far worse than a cliff. I was headed toward a burning Hell.

My mother and grandmother were both very religious. I didn't think I would ever be good enough to be saved if I had to reach the level of religiosity that they had. So, at that time I just figured I wasn't good enough to be a real Christian (although, to be honest, I wasn't too concerned about it either way). My idea of Christianity was extremely worldly, and not at all Biblical.

Pastor Morrow didn't seem like one of the worldly hypocrites who ignored sin, yet he said, "Jesus paid it all." He didn't say anything that led me to believe he lived like the Devil, but he still said that my obedience and good works didn't contribute to my own salvation in any way.

25

There was something very real and very sincere about him. It was like he had one hundred percent confidence in what he was saying, and he really cared about me, even though he barely knew me.

For the first time (that I could remember anyway) I had met a Christian man who didn't seem to be a hypocrite, but who also said there is freedom in Christ — that Christ paid it all!

At that point in time, I had no spiritual desire at all. I was perfectly content in the world. My primary focus was on making money and providing for my family. Yet, our conversation that day would stick with me for years to come. A seed was planted in my heart that day, although it would lie dormant for several years.

- 3 -

The Wakeup Call

"Why do we even exist?"

After my conversation with Pastor Morrow, I went right back to the life I was living. I drank. I smoked. I cursed. I satisfied every passion I could. I obsessed over my online business and how I could make more money. I was very apathetic towards the world and any kind of suffering that anyone was going through.

During this time, if I heard about a child who was abused (or some other sad story) I was able to just completely ignore it, like it wasn't real. I did that for many years to live in my own little self-indulgent, sinful world where my happiness and my feelings were the most important things. I didn't think I needed a savior because I didn't think there was anything I needed to be saved from. I didn't need God because I had myself!

Morally I was at an all-time low and as apathetic as ever. I was also as far from God as ever. I remember telling my mother around this time that I believed the Bible was just a book and that, being just a book, it probably had changed many times throughout the years.

In hindsight, I realize that my opinion grew from my hope that it wasn't true. At that time, I knew that if it was true, I would be in big trouble on the Day of Judgment!

After living in Evansville for a year, we moved into a nicer apartment on the Southside of Indianapolis. My wife, Claudia, is from Germany and she had some German friends in the Indianapolis area. We also wanted more things to do. We wanted a more active life than what we'd had in southern Indiana. Little did I know that shortly after moving there, I would be faced with something that would shake my world and force me to step outside of my self-made bubble for the first time in my life.

For several years, my older brother, Matt, had been dealing with various health issues. Out of nowhere he would just black out. He had dizzy spells from time to time. Half of his body would go numb frequently. He had seizures on more than one occasion, among other things. These issues caused me to worry about him to a certain extent, but for the most part, I went on with my life unaffected.

That was until he came up to Indianapolis one morning with his girlfriend, our mother, and one of our sisters, for an appointment with a new neurologist, who was said to be one of the leading neurologists in the state.

We all drove to the IU Medical Center for the appointment. After a great deal of time waiting nervously, packed into a small exam room, the doctor finally came in. He had reviewed all of Matt's previous scans and overall history, and he had a diagnosis. It was the worst possible news. He diagnosed Matt with a brain tumor that he believed was situated near the center of his brain and would be inoperable due to its location.

We were all devastated. I went home that day, locked myself in my bedroom, and wept. I couldn't ignore this one. My sinful vices weren't enough to conquer this one. I had never dealt with the loss of anyone close to me aside from grandparents and a cousin.

I loved my grandparents and cousin, but this was completely different. Although my brother and I weren't super close, so to speak, we were brothers. At that time, I could count on two hands the number of people who meant a lot to me, and he was one of them. I grew up with him and loved him, and now I thought he would soon be gone forever.

I remember asking Claudia, "What is the purpose of life if we all just die? Why are we even here?" I believe her answer was, "That's the big question. That's what everyone wants to know."

That day, for the first time in my life, I felt like I needed to read the Bible. Although I had previously made the statement that "the Bible is just a book that has probably changed" I knew deep down in my heart that it was special. I looked around but couldn't find one. So, I got in the car and drove to a bookstore so I could buy one. It was a cheap, basic KJV Bible with no maps, notes, references, or anything, and I didn't care. I just wanted to see if it would answer my questions.

That same day, I remember standing alone in front of the bathroom mirror of our apartment, weeping. I stood there and prayed. I remember begging God to heal my brother. I remember making a promise to God that if He would heal my brother, I would make changes in my life.

The next day the doctor read the results of the new scan that was done when we were there. The shape of what was thought to be a tumor had changed, and it was much smaller. It was not a tumor! Matt was eventually diagnosed with having had strokes and, by God's grace, my brother is still with us as I write this.

I do not believe that it was my "If you'll do this then I'll do that" prayer that caused God to work that miracle. But it was certainly a direct answer to the many prayers we all prayed. I don't know how God works His miracles. Maybe it was a tumor and He healed Matt or maybe He worked in some other way, but I just thank Him that my big brother is still with us today!

Matt had several more ups and downs with his health after that. He is still unable to hold a full-time job because of the effects of the strokes he has suffered, but he is with us and able to live a normal life. We thank God for that!

After the day that we thought Matt was going to pass away, things changed for me mentally, spiritually and emotionally. The ability that I'd had before to just block out the evil and suffering in the world was gone. Now if I heard of a child starving to death, it would tear me up inside. If I imagined my son being diagnosed with a horrible disease, it would cause me to worry like never before.

I remember watching the news and realizing that people are killed, tortured, seriously injured, and suffer in all kinds of horrible ways. I also remembered that society as a whole couldn't care less! People will say a nice word, put on a sad face, and maybe shake their head. But give them thirty seconds and they've already forgotten! It made me realize just how insignificant I was to the world and how insignificant most people are to the rest of society.

If I died today, the world would go on as if I had never existed. That's not to say that my loved ones wouldn't care. Of course, they would. But overall, my life means absolutely nothing to most people in the world. That is a fact that I had not previously realized.

Life wasn't all fun and games anymore. Life was serious. After nearly thirty years of living in the moment, I began to seriously consider what happens when we die. I wondered where I would spend eternity. For these reasons I began to read the Bible and pray on a regular basis.

- 4 -

"Kicking Against the Goad"

Acts 26:14 *"It is hard for thee to kick against the pricks."*

When the apostle Paul (then Saul) was met by the Lord Jesus as he walked to Damascus to persecute Christians, the Lord said to him "Saul, Saul, why persecutest thou me? It is hard for thee to kick against the pricks."

The analogy was familiar to any Jew at that time. A farmer would guide his oxen with an "ox goad." This was a stick with a sharp iron tip that was used to steer the ox. Occasionally an ox would kick back at the goad in rebellion, resulting in a more severe prodding. So, it was hard for the ox to "kick against the pricks."

Saul was a deeply religious Jew, a Pharisee. The Pharisees were religious leaders during the time of the Lord Jesus' earthly ministry. They despised Christians. It was the Pharisees who handed our Lord over to the Roman authorities and demanded that He be crucified. Christ rebuked the Pharisees for offering their "good works" and self-righteousness to the Lord. They added their own traditions apart from God's Word. They required all the Israelites to keep these man-made laws. They rigorously kept these laws, while holding back their hearts from God.

33

Saul had a mission to arrest as many Christians as he could and that was what he was going to Damascus to do. But the Lord had other plans for him.

Christ had apparently been working on Saul's conscience. Saul had likely heard many of the teachings of Christ. They were prodding him - goading him. But through his rejection of Christ and his zeal in persecuting Christians, he kept "kicking against the pricks." That is until he encountered Christ. What a day!

From that day forward he dropped his Hebrew name "Saul" (meaning "desired") and picked up his Greek name "Paul" (meaning "little"). He was converted! He no longer lived to gain favor and honor for himself. He now lived for Christ in humility.

> **2 Corinthians 5:17,** "Therefore if any man be in Christ, he is a new creature: old things are passed away; behold, all things are become new."

After my brother Matt's misdiagnosis, like Saul, I was kicking against the pricks for several years. I continued to read God's Word, though not daily, and sometimes not even weekly. I knew that I was living in sin, yet I was not willing to repent of it.

I had broken the promise I made to God the day of Matt's tumor diagnosis. I had promised to change if He would heal him. I was just like a child who doesn't want to do the work if he is paid ahead of time, or who just plain wants his way. One thing had changed though. I was no longer able to block out the evils of the world.

I loved sin just as much as before, but over time, as the Lord started to shine His light on me, my love for sin began to prick my conscience like it never did before. Verses like 1 Corinthians 6:9-10 would prick my heart.

> **1 Corinthians 6:9-10,** "Know ye not that the unrighteous shall not inherit the kingdom of God? Be not deceived: neither fornicators, nor idolaters, nor adulterers, nor effeminate, nor abusers of themselves with mankind, Nor thieves, nor covetous, nor drunkards, nor revilers, nor extortioners, shall inherit the kingdom of God."

From time to time, I would release a big "kick" so to speak, by embracing sin in one extreme way or another. For a day or two I would get comfort, but when I did this, I always ended up even more miserable than before. I was doing the same thing that Saul had done, but in a different scenario.

I began to desperately seek meaning in life. I was reading the Bible, but I didn't understand much of it at that point. Although I felt drawn to the Bible and began to feel guilty about my sin, I didn't really know what I believed.

I remember going outside at night in the summer, after Claudia and my son were in bed. I couldn't sleep. I remember looking into the night sky on many occasions, seeing the moon and the stars, and just knowing deep down that there was something more that I didn't have. There was something missing inside, and I knew it. I really knew it.

During this same period, I began to get into politics. Although I knew that dishonest, unethical people were embedded in every political party, I began to realize that our country, and the world, was not making progress — not by any definition of progress that I considered important. On the contrary, I saw society growing more and more evil by the day. This social and moral decay, which does not seem to be easing up, really ate away at me for several years.

In August of 2012 my second son, Clayton, was born. Clayton was born with a cleft soft pallet, so we knew that he would have to undergo surgery around his first birthday. That caused me to worry about a variety of things such as him getting anesthesia at such a young age, or the potential for severe speech problems, among other issues.

Around the same time, I decided to sell most of my profitable business assets (for no good reason other than to have a nice lump sum of money). I thought I could easily replicate them all. That didn't happen.

My income dropped considerably. The cash from the sale was gone quicker than I expected. Now, on top of the other stresses of life, I was racking up credit card debt as I desperately scrambled to rebuild my online business.

By this time, I was also as desperate as ever to find meaning in the craziness of life. I was reading my Bible just about every day and praying like never before. It was during this time that I started to realize I wasn't a condemned sinner just because of my "bad sins," I was condemned because of my "little sins" too.

> **John 3:18,** "He that believeth on him is not condemned: but he that believeth not is condemned already...

God's condemnation of sinful man (of ... *me*) began to settle in at this time. I began to *really* believe what the Bible said about sin.

The guilt became heavier and heavier as I discovered videos online from preachers and evangelists, like Paul Washer, who laid out the problem of sin and the need of a "rebirth" very plainly.

> **John 3:3,** "Jesus answered and said unto him, Verily, ver-
> ily, I say unto thee, Except a man be born again, he cannot
> see the kingdom of God."

Through these men God began to crush my spirit, reveal-
ing to me the truth of my own sinfulness.

I realized that anything besides perfection is sin. I
had told countless lies (even the "little white" lies are sin).
That made me a liar. I had taken things that didn't belong
to me. They seemed small before, but that made me a
thief. I had used God's name in vain; that made me a
blasphemer. I had committed sexual sins (in Matthew
5:28, Jesus said even having impure thoughts about someone is the same as the physical act); that made me an
adulterer and fornicator. I'd had hateful thoughts towards
others, and that made me a murderer by the standards of
our perfect God (Matthew 5:21-22).

I realized that although I sincerely believed I was a
good person for the most part, in fact I was a liar, a thief,
a blasphemer, a fornicator, and even a murderer (among
other things) before Holy God. My conscience agreed
with most of this.

My standard of goodness was flawed because of my
fallen, sinful nature. But God is not flawed. His standard
is infinitely higher than mine. So, by reading the Bible, I
began to understand that I wasn't nearly as good as I'd
thought I was. If I had died at that time and stood before
our perfect, Holy God, I would have been rightly condemned. If I had died and stood before Him, and He let
me go, He would not have been good! He would have
been like a bad judge.

At this point I was heavily convicted of my sin. At
the same time, I unbelievably continued to go out of my
way to commit some sins. I was so in bondage to sin that

I was near the breaking point. I don't think I've ever really been suicidal in my life, but whatever the condition is before suicidal tendencies, that's where I was.

Then on December 14, 2012, news started to spread about the mass murder of twenty children. A man had entered a school building and began murdering little children. Twenty children and six adult staff members were murdered that day. I had two little boys, and one was in grade school, so this was the final crushing blow to my spirit.

I began to think about those little kids and how horrified they must have been. I thought of the families who were probably just being notified that their precious little children were just murdered. I began to obsessively worry about my boys. What if something like this happened to them? What if one of my boys got cancer? What if we got in an accident? Worry on top of worry flooded my thoughts.

Shortly after, I had an anxiety attack for the first time in my life. I had horrible insomnia. I went as many as four days without any sleep at all on more than one occasion. I was a complete mess mentally, physically, and spiritually.

On top of the tragedy, the media, and government officials, began to use the deaths of these children for political gain to push foolish and dangerous agendas. It was like my entire world was tumbling down around me. I was ready to give up.

I realized I needed some spiritual guidance, but I wasn't in touch with a single preacher. So, I started thinking about someone who might be able to help me. I quickly thought about Pastor Michael Morrow, whom I had spoken to all those years before. I remembered that I had added him as a friend on Facebook a while back, so I found him there and sent him a message. He was quick to respond, and he began to feed me spiritually. He gave me the gospel again.

I was heavily convicted of my sin. I was trying to quit sinning because that's what I thought I had to do. I figured if God is good, then I had better stop sinning. The problem was that no matter how hard I tried, I couldn't. I really tried not to sin, but one way or another, whether in thought or action, I would eventually catch myself sinning.

I sent Pastor Morrow a message and asked him if he ever sinned. After looking through our online conversation again recently, I am amazed how blind I was. He gave me the perfect answers from God's Word. But somehow, I just didn't get it at first. We messaged back and forth for several days, and he gave me a great deal of wise counsel during those days. God used that counsel to lead to the most amazing day of my entire life: December 19, 2012.

- 5 -

The Day God Touched Me

Matthew 8:2-3 *"And, behold, there came a leper and worshipped him, saying, Lord, if thou wilt, thou canst make me clean. And Jesus put forth his hand, and touched him, saying, I will; be thou clean. And immediately his leprosy was cleansed."*

After Christ preached the Sermon on the Mount, a man with leprosy came to Him. This leper was unlike many of the other people who were following Him. Many other people weren't following the Lord because they had a real need. They were following Him to see miracles and other great things.

Perhaps some thought that by following Him they would gain His favor. This leper, though, had a big problem. According to the law, leprosy made a man ceremonially unclean. If a man came into contact with a leper, that man also became unclean. This man was unclean spiritually, physically, and ceremonially. He *needed* help.

This leper came to Christ with a big problem. He had no doubt that he had this problem, and he had no doubt that the Lord was able to cure him of it. The leper didn't try to deny that he was a leper in need of a cure. He completely believed that the Lord Jesus was his only hope. Because of his faith, the Lord healed him!

> **Matthew 8:3,** "And Jesus put forth his hand, and touched him, saying, I will; be thou clean. And immediately his leprosy was cleansed."

I was just like that leper. I didn't have physical leprosy, but I did have spiritual leprosy. I was unclean because of my sin. I needed help and Christ was the only one who could help me. Just like that leper, I came to the Lord with my problem. I didn't come to Him pleading that I wasn't too bad of a person. I came to Him in complete honesty, admitting in my heart that I was a dirty sinner who needed undeserved grace! I *knew* I was lost.

On the cold winter day of December 19, 2012, five days after the school murders and after communicating with Pastor Morrow for several days, I finally got to the end of myself. I finally realized and accepted that I was a sinner and that there was nothing I could do about it. I *knew* I was lost. I finally just quit trying to be strong and admitted my weakness and inability to meet God's perfect standard.

On that day, I lay in my bed weeping in desperation. I believed intellectually that the Bible was true. I believed there was a God. I believed that Jesus Christ was the Son of God. I also believed the Bible was God's Word. But mine was just blind, intellectual faith. There was no reality to it. I needed more than that and I knew it.

I was completely empty inside. I prayed regularly, I was trying hard not to sin, and I asked God to help me, but the misery remained. I was lost.

Anxiety and worries raced through my mind. My sin weighed on me like a ton of bricks. The wickedness of the world terrified me. The future of my children terrified me. The future of our country terrified me. Christ's words about sin and judgment terrified me. I was . . . terrified.

That morning I lay down in my bed with my pillow over my face, and I prayed the most desperate prayer of my life. I was sick of it all. I was sick of the cruel world, worrying about finances, worrying about the future of my children, and worrying about God's holy judgment on me because of my sin. I was lost.

As I laid there weeping, I begged God to take my soul. I wasn't suicidal. I wasn't asking Him to take my life, but I was asking, no, begging, Him to forcefully take over my soul — to claim my soul, my life — to be His and His alone right then and forevermore. I remember specifically saying to Him, "Just take it! It's yours, just take it!" I also remember telling Him that I had nothing to offer but sin.

I admitted to Him that I was just a filthy sinner who couldn't stop sinning, as much as I really did try. I didn't know the theology behind what I was asking. All I knew was that I needed something more than what I had. I needed something that I didn't deserve. I needed grace! I had a gaping hole in my heart, and I needed the God of the universe to fill it.

Nothing happened immediately after that prayer. I went on with the day, trying to overcome the anxiety and guilt and get some work done. I knew that sin was the main problem, so I figured that it was my sin that was keeping God from taking this all from me. But my problem was that I *couldn't* stop sinning. This sin guilt caused me to get online and do a Google search for "how to overcome sin." I found an article (which no longer appears in Google for that search query) that pointed me to Romans 6-7. The article explained the passages, but I had to see them for myself. I opened my Bible and turned there.

Romans 6:23, "For the wages of sin is death; but the gift of God is eternal life through Jesus Christ our Lord.

Romans 7:15-25, "For that which I do, I allow not: for what I would, that do I not; but what I hate, that do I.

If then I do that which I would not, I consent unto the law that it is good.

Now then it is no more I that do it, but sin that dwelleth in me.

For I know that in me (that is, in my flesh,) dwelleth no good thing: for to will is present with me; but how to perform that which is good I find not.

For the good that I would, I do not: but the evil which I would not, that I do.

Now if I do that I would not, it is no more I that do it, but sin that dwelleth in me.

I find then a law, that, when I would do good, evil is present with me.

For I delight in the law of God after the inward man:

But I see another law in my members, warring against the law of my mind, and bringing me into captivity to the law of sin which is in my members.

O wretched man that I am! Who shall deliver me from the body of this death?

I thank God through Jesus Christ our Lord. So then with the mind I myself serve the law of God; but with the flesh the law of sin."

> **Romans 8:1,** "There is therefore now no condemnation to them which are in Christ Jesus, who walk not after the flesh, but after the Spirit."

I didn't understand many of the details that the apostle Paul provided in these chapters. But I did understand one thing: Paul was a sinner. Even as he wrote the Scriptures, Paul was a sinner. Paul had the same sin problem that I had. He hated his sin and didn't want to sin (he was penitent) but he was still a sinner. What was his solution? Jesus Christ!

"There is therefore now *no condemnation* . . ." This told me that it was not about *my* goodness, it was about *Christ's* goodness. I realized at that point that "*He* paid it all" just like Pastor Morrow had said all of those years before. When Jesus Christ hung from that cross and cried out, "It is finished," it truly was *finished*!

> **John 19:30,** "When Jesus therefore had received the vinegar, he said, It is finished: and he bowed his head, and gave up the ghost."

When I realized that I am not condemned because of what Christ did for me on the cross, I finally believed in my heart. I had believed intellectually before this, but this was different. *In that instant, the most indescribable, amazing, heart-warming, freeing peace I had ever felt in my life penetrated my entire being! It was like God literally reached down from Heaven and touched me. It was like He wrapped His arms around me and said "Your sins are forgiven. You now belong to me."*

I knew, at that moment, that Jesus Christ was *my* Lord and that I had just been born again. I was forgiven! I felt the deepest, warmest love I had ever felt; both toward God and toward my fellow man. I felt like I could forgive anyone, and I had a real desire to hug everyone I came across (though I'm glad I didn't). I wanted to scream out of the window, "It's real! The Bible is true! Christ IS the Way, the Truth, and the Life!"

> **John 3:3,** "Jesus answered and said unto him, Verily, verily, I say unto thee, Except a man be born again, he cannot see the kingdom of God."

I immediately sent Pastor Morrow a message. The exact words I used were "I GET IT! MAN, I feel . . . SAVED!!!" It was very real, and I knew for a fact that my sin had been forgiven.

Before this I didn't think much about being "born again." It was really just another religious phrase to me. I didn't realize there was a *reality* to it. I didn't know you could *know* for *sure* that you were born again.

> **2 Corinthians 1:22,** "Who hath also sealed us, and given the earnest of the Spirit in our hearts."

Although Pastor Morrow had given me the gospel on several occasions, and even his salvation testimony the first time we met, the truth and reality of "moment-in-time salvation" (the reality of being born again) just wasn't something that stuck with me.

A few years after the Lord saved me, Pastor Morrow told me his testimony again and it was exactly in line with what had happened to me. Before the Lord saved me, I just knew that something was missing. From Scripture I could see that my sin separated me from God.

After I was born again, my mind was immediately flooded with realizations. I realized what the lyrics to the song "Amazing Grace" meant (and many other hymns)! "I once was lost, but now I'm found, was blind but now I see. How precious did that grace appear the hour I first believed!"

I was also franticly reading through the Scriptures again, with my eyes wide open, going through passage after passage that now had new meaning!

> **Matthew 13:10-13,** "And the disciples came, and said unto him, Why speakest thou unto them in parables?
>
> He answered and said unto them, Because it is given unto you to know the mysteries of the kingdom of heaven, but to them it is not given.
>
> For whosoever hath, to him shall be given, and he shall have more abundance: but whosoever hath not, from him shall be taken away even that he hath.
>
> Therefore speak I to them in parables: because they seeing see not; and hearing they hear not, neither do they understand."

The day the Lord saved me I sent Pastor Morrow a message telling him that I had been born again (we had been exchanging messages on Facebook for several days by this time and I was in an emotional frenzy).

Because my rebirth experience was so dramatic, I felt like no-one could possibly understand this peace that passes understanding. I remember being a little surprised at how Pastor Morrow responded. He responded with joy, but it was as if he had heard of this experience many times. He knew exactly what I was talking about. I didn't have to explain, because he had been saved decades before, and had witnessed countless others who had since then.

He connected me with a good friend of his, Pastor Rob Pelkey, who pastored a church near me. He told me that Pastor Pelkey said that I could call him anytime I wanted, even if it was 3:00 a.m.

Since my conversion, I felt loved more than I ever had in my life, and I felt far greater love for others. I felt like hugging everyone I came across.

This love created a heavy burden for the lost. I wanted to tell everyone what had happened. I wanted to urge them to repent and believe the gospel.

> **Mark 1:14-15,** "Now after that John was put in prison, Jesus came into Galilee, preaching the gospel of the kingdom of God,
>
> And saying, The time is fulfilled, and the kingdom of God is at hand: repent ye, and believe the gospel."

That burden weighed heavily on me after my conversion. I went through times of extreme joy for what the Lord had done for me, but also times of extreme pain and sorrow for those I loved that I believed to be lost.

One day shortly after Pastor Morrow had given me Pastor Pelkey's phone number, I was lying in bed not able to sleep. The undeniable reality of God's Word that I now knew as fact, included the truth that all who are not born again are already condemned.

> **John 3:18,** "He that believeth on him is not condemned: but he that believeth not is condemned already, because he

hath not believed in the name of the only begotten Son of God."

John 3:3, "Jesus answered and said unto him, Verily, verily, I say unto thee, Except a man be born again, he cannot see the kingdom of God."

As I laid there worrying about lost loved ones, among other things that crept into my mind, due to my lack of overall knowledge, I decided to hold Pastor Pelkey to his word. It was the middle of the night, and I called him.

He answered and was not upset at all. In fact, he seemed happy that I called. He asked a few questions about what was going on. As I began to explain, he started filling in the blanks, but not because Pastor Morrow had told him all the details (I'm pretty sure he had not).

Things I forgot to mention, he already knew. It was like he was there when it happened. I was amazed! He knew exactly what I was talking about because he had also been saved many years before.

It was a blessing to speak with someone who had experienced the same thing! He prayed with me over the phone and shared both my extreme joy and grief. He really cared about my troubles and truly rejoiced in my salvation. There was nothing fake about him and I knew it.

Then Pastor Pelkey began to ease my mind with truths from God's Word. He explained that the peace I felt at that point in time was God (in the person of the Holy Spirit) literally coming into my heart. It was more than just a "hug" from God, so to speak. He explained that I now belonged to Christ for eternity. He showed me that my burden for the lost was a good thing and that it was put there by God Himself. He explained that God loves my loved ones more than I love them.

Pastor Pelkey helped me to see that, although each individual person must repent and trust in Christ for himself, the Lord is already moving toward saving the family of each believer. Now they have someone close to pray for them.

Although I continued to have much discomfort over the burden of lost loved ones, Pastor Pelkey's phone conversation and prayers provided much comfort.

Over time I met more Christians who shared their testimonies of saving faith, which greatly blessed me. I also found many salvation testimonies online from people who had been born again. The many salvation testimonies that I've heard, and continue to come across, are an incredible blessing. I can never hear a salvation testimony without rejoicing in the Lord for what He has done.

Many churches today preach the true biblical doctrine of salvation. But I often wonder what goes through the minds of those church goers who hear the truth of conversion but have never had a day in their life when they knew personally that their sin had been forgiven, and that they were born again. How are they content to go on with life as usual, with no real assurance of salvation, knowing they could die at any moment with no second chance?

I imagine that many of those people think that salvation testimonies like mine are just the result of an adrenalin rush, or the good feeling you have after a good cry, or something else that is easily explained away.

If they only knew the reality of it though, they would tremble at the thought that there was never a day when their own salvation was a reality — that they themselves may be one to whom the Lord Jesus finally says, "I never knew you: depart from Me."

> **Matthew 7:23,** "And then will I profess unto them, I never knew you: depart from me, ye that work iniquity."

Although Pastor Morrow did tell me his salvation testimony all of those years ago, the point in time of salvation (being born again), for whatever reason, didn't stick in my memory.

When the Lord saved me on that cold December evening, the only reason that I knew I was born again was because *God made it known to me*. I wasn't going to church, and I wasn't striving to be religious. I just knew that I needed God to fill the emptiness in my soul, and I knew that my sin separated me from Him. *I knew I was lost.*

Now, by His grace, because of the blood of Jesus Christ, I am no longer separated from Him. I rejoice in that. At the same time, I am praying that many more will be saved.

- 6 -

Learning to Walk

Romans 8:29 *"For whom he did foreknow, he also did predestinate to be conformed to the image of his Son, that he might be the firstborn among many brethren."*

After becoming a Christian that day, I was full of joy, nearly non-stop, for almost a year. That same joy that came into my heart the moment I first believed, stayed there *almost* constantly. No matter what the circumstances, I was full of joy. Like King David, I wanted to tell everyone what the Lord had done for me!

> **Psalm 66:16,** "Come and hear, all ye that fear God, and I will declare what he hath done for my soul."

Along with that joy I had an incredible zeal to proclaim the gospel. In many cases that zeal resulted in gospel seeds being planted. But in other cases, because of my own immaturity, I'm afraid I caused some people to stumble.

At the time I had little knowledge of who God was. I knew the most basic form of the gospel: that I was a condemned sinner and that Christ paid it all for me (I was saved on that day because I believed that in my heart). But beyond that, despite all the Bible reading I had done in the previous years, I had very little knowledge. This was because I was spiritually blind before I was saved.

> **2 Corinthians 4:3-6,** "But if our gospel be hid, it is hid to them that are lost:
>
> In whom the god of this world hath blinded the minds of them which believe not, lest the light of the glorious gospel of Christ, who is the image of God, should shine unto them.
>
> For we preach not ourselves, but Christ Jesus the Lord; and ourselves your servants for Jesus' sake.
>
> For God, who commanded the light to shine out of darkness, hath shined in our hearts, to give the light of the knowledge of the glory of God in the face of Jesus Christ."

A heart that is on fire for the Lord, combined with a mind that has very little knowledge of the Lord, can have unintended consequences. I did not choose my words so wisely! In many cases the truths that I did speak were spoken in the wrong way. Mixed in with those truths were many things that were just simply wrong. I had good intentions, but as a brand-new believer I had not yet learned that it is God's Word that has power, not mine. I also needed to learn that any ideas of truth that are not firmly rooted in Scripture are worthless imaginations.

As a new believer, I had to learn that, although I had been adopted into God's family through Christ (justified because of the righteousness of Christ, my substitute), I had just begun my walk. I had just met Christ, and I needed to get to know Him better each day.

Believers are counted righteous judicially the moment they are saved. However, they are progressively being saved from the effects of sin, and being conformed to His image, daily.

> **Romans 8:29,** "For whom he did foreknow, he also did predestinate to be conformed to the image of his Son, that he might be the firstborn among many brethren."

Along with my lack of overall knowledge was a lack of complete repentance. Although I knew my past, present, and future sin had been forgiven (nailed to that cross), I had a new sense of guilt. My previous guilt had been tied closely to God's wrath and my rightful condemnation as a sinner. That guilt was completely gone! This new guilt was tied closely to God's love! I desired to please Him, and when I sinned, I sinned against my loving Savior, who is Holy and still hates sin.

My sin guilt went from a fear of condemnation to a fear of letting down someone close to me. He bled and died on that cross (and that's just the beginning of His sufferings on that cross) for *me* because of *my* sin. How could I still go on sinning against Him?

I knew for a fact that I had been forgiven. I knew that this forgiveness was forever. I knew that my position, in Christ, was eternally settled the moment I repented and believed the gospel.

> **John 10:27-30,** "My sheep hear my voice, and I know them, and they follow me: And I give unto them eternal life; and they shall never perish, neither shall any man pluck them out of my hand. My Father, which gave them me, is greater than all; and no man is able to pluck them out of my Father's hand. I and my Father are one."

However, I didn't see this as a "free ticket" to sin. I couldn't see it as such. I had literally been changed from within! I didn't want to keep on sinning. I was more penitent than ever; it just wasn't the victory I longed for. I had been shown mercy from the very God whom I had sinned against for all those years. I had a new heart with new desires. But I still had the "old self" in me that longed for sin.

Like a drug addict who realizes that the drugs are killing him, I knew that my lingering sins had to be conquered if I were to grow spiritually and live a peaceful and productive life for the Lord.

I had a deepened reverence for living for my Lord, and more repentance than I had previously, but my conversion didn't instantly cure me completely of all sin desire. It did, however, create in me a deepened desire to overcome my sin and have a clear conscience. I now have a very real desire to work out my daily salvation from the power of sin out of love for and obedience to Christ, who saved me!

> **Philippians 2:12,** "... work out your own salvation with fear and trembling."

The good news is that I had something that a drug addict doesn't have. I had God Himself literally living inside me. I was, and am, literally possessed by God!

To this day, though I certainly have had instances of backsliding, the Holy Spirit continues to work in me to overcome those sin addictions as I "take up my cross" every day.

> **Matthew 16:24,** "Then said Jesus unto his disciples, If any man will come after me, let him deny himself, and take up his cross, and follow me."

When the Lord spoke these words, He wasn't saying that the life of His disciples must be a painful, sorrowful, miserable existence. He was saying that we are to deny ourselves and live for Him. If we are living in sin, we are doing just the opposite. I quickly learned that, as a believer, if I did *not* pick up my cross and live for Him, I would be miserable! This is just the opposite of what I used to think that verse implied. It is impossible for a true Christian to embrace sin without being miserable inside.

I had honestly tried, *very* hard, to overcome sin previously, but I just couldn't. Now I could! I wasn't, and certainly am not, perfect. But I have victory. I know I will not be completely free from sin until I am with Him in glory, but by the power of the Holy Spirit who lives within me, I no longer embrace that sin. Sin no longer rules me!

> **Romans 6:8-14,** "Now if we be dead with Christ, we believe that we shall also live with him:
>
> Knowing that Christ being raised from the dead dieth no more; death hath no more dominion over him.
>
> For in that he died, he died unto sin once: but in that he liveth, he liveth unto God.
>
> Likewise reckon ye also yourselves to be dead indeed unto sin, but alive unto God through Jesus Christ our Lord.

Let not sin therefore reign in your mortal body, that ye should obey it in the lusts thereof.

Neither yield ye your members as instruments of unrighteousness unto sin: but yield yourselves unto God, as those that are alive from the dead, and your members as instruments of righteousness unto God.

For sin shall not have dominion over you: for ye are not under the law, but under grace."

- 7 -

Rethinking the Local Church

Hebrews 10:25 *"Not forsaking the assembling of ourselves together, as the manner of some is; but exhorting one another: and so much the more, as ye see the day approaching."*

For most of my adult life, I had a very negative attitude toward local churches. Many of the churches that I had visited previously were full of people who I believed to be hypocrites who thought they were better than everyone else. I put them all in the same bucket, so to speak, and labeled them all as religious hypocrites.

Even after I was saved, for eight months or so, I came up with one excuse after another not to attend a local church, though in my heart I truly desired to be in a good church.

I attended Pastor Pelkey's church for one service shortly after the Lord saved me. But even though I knew that Pastor Pelkey was not one of the hypocrites that I imagined filled the churches of America, I remained out of church for eight months. The desire that the Lord put in my heart for fellowship with other Christians, however, soon overtook me. I was hungry to learn from them and to grow.

I knew that God's Word contained everything that I needed to grow spiritually and to walk with the Lord.

59

> **2 Timothy 3:16-17,** "All scripture is given by inspiration of God, and is profitable for doctrine, for reproof, for correction, for instruction in righteousness: That the man of God may be perfect, thoroughly furnished unto all good works."

But I also knew that God used men to preach and to teach.

> **2 Timothy 4:1-2,** "I charge thee therefore before God, and the Lord Jesus Christ, who shall judge the quick and the dead at his appearing and his kingdom;
>
> Preach the word; be instant in season, out of season; reprove, rebuke, exhort with all long suffering and doctrine."
>
> **Romans 10:13-15,** "For whosoever shall call upon the name of the Lord shall be saved.
>
> How then shall they call on him in whom they have not believed? And how shall they believe in him of whom they have not heard? And how shall they hear without a preacher?
>
> And how shall they preach, except they be sent? As it is written, How beautiful are the feet of them that preach the gospel of peace, and bring glad tidings of good things!"

I eventually knew it was time to get over myself, to rise above any self-righteousness or hypocrisy that I might run into, and to get into a local, Bible-believing church. I desired fellowship with other Christians, and I wanted to join others in really worshipping Christ. I also had an incredible desire to learn, so I was seeking a good pastor to mentor me.

The first church that came to mind was Sherwood Hills Baptist Church, the church that Brother Pelkey pastored. This is a small Baptist church on the east side of Indianapolis. I had visited there once shortly after the Lord saved me. There weren't many more than twenty or thirty people who attended on any given Sunday, but this church was like no other that I had been to. There was real love there. People were happy to be there, and they seemed to just be happy in general!

Many of the members had salvation testimonies just like mine. They spoke of a moment when the burden of their sin was lifted, and peace came into their hearts. There was a reality to it, just like there was with my own moment of salvation.

It wasn't just a social club or a religious group. Pastor Pelkey preached with passion. It was all *real* to him and to the members of the church. Everything he preached just seemed right and was in line with the little knowledge of the Scriptures that I did have.

That church was twenty minutes from my home though. That meant I would be driving for forty minutes, on top of the time I spent there. That would not have been a problem, not even a consideration, if it weren't for the fact that Claudia, my wife, was not yet attending church. This was all new to her. I didn't want to start spending a great deal of time in church, away from her and the boys (knowing that she wasn't ready to start attending a church at that time). Because of this, I decided to look for a church closer to our home.

I visited another church that was close to home, and I was greeted very kindly. The preacher preached a good message, but it just wasn't the same as Pastor Pelkey's preaching. I decided to go back to that church for a Sunday evening Bible Study. I was the only one who showed up, aside from the pastor and the assistant pastor. The assistant pastor, who had apparently pastored his own church for decades, was teaching the Bible Study.

I began to tell him how the Lord had saved me, and a little bit about myself. As I was speaking, he walked out of the room to check on something. I couldn't help but think about how rude that was. He might as well have just said, "I really don't care what you have to say."

I was respectful for the rest of the Bible Study, but as I'm sure you can imagine, I never went back to that church. One phrase that I do remember him saying was, "Some people are saved out of sin and others are saved from sin. I was saved from sin. I never got into sin like many others." I was immediately concerned after hearing that statement (and seeing the apathy that his actions suggested). His statement brought a verse to mind. The verse in Ecclesiastes that the apostle Paul referenced in his letter to the Romans:

> **Ecclesiastes 7:20,** "For there is not a just man upon earth, that doeth good, and sinneth not."

I did not let that experience keep me from seeking a solid Bible-preaching church. I looked up several other churches that were close to home. Several of them published the preacher's sermons online, so I listened to many of those. A couple of them sounded doctrinally correct, but I wasn't drawn to any of those churches.

At this point I turned to the Lord in prayer (I should have done that to begin with. He is not a last resort; He is Sovereign God over all the affairs of the heavens and earth.) I prayed that He would guide me to just the right church. The church that He wanted me in. A church that preached the uncompromised gospel and that stood on God's Word. My heart craved a church with members who had genuine love for one another and testimonies of real salvation!

The Lord said that all men will know His disciples by their love.

> **John 13:35,** "By this shall all men know that ye are my disciples, if ye have love one to another."

So, I prayed He would guide me to them. I knew if He would save me, then He would also send me to a good church if I asked.

Immediately after I prayed, it was like the Lord was saying "I told you where I wanted you after I saved you." I knew at that moment that He had sent me to Pastor Pelkey and his flock at Sherwood Hills Baptist Church, so that's exactly where I went.

Shortly after I began attending the church, I was baptized, becoming a member. Claudia had seen the change in my life since I was saved, and would be years later before she got saved, she began going to church with me as well!

My previous bias about church was gone after I started attending. Joining that church and being baptized seemed as natural as going to sleep at night. Believers should be in church growing, having fellowship, and worshiping together. I felt at home there.

I was disobedient in waiting so long to join a Bible believing church and in waiting so long to be Scripturally baptized (which is a local church ordinance). I was baptized as a child, but I was never Scripturally baptized. Scriptural baptism is a public profession of an inward change (salvation). It is the "believers" baptism. I was aware that the water baptism would not do anything as far as adding to my salvation. I knew that I was already saved "by grace, through faith."

> **Ephesians 2:8-9,** "For by grace are ye saved through faith; and that not of yourselves: it is the gift of God: Not of works, lest any man should boast."

But I also knew Christians were told to make that profession public after being born again. This would testify to our own spiritual death, burial, and resurrection with Christ. I had waited about nine months to do that, which was too long.

Over the next few years, I learned a great deal from my pastor and the church. Not only did I acquire knowledge, but more importantly I learned to walk with the Lord (after all these years later I know that this process of growth doesn't end until we go to be with Him). I began to be rooted deeper in Christ, and to know more about the One who loved me and gave Himself for me.

One can have degrees in theology, know the Bible front to back intellectually, and still not know God. Knowing God and knowing about God are two profoundly different things. I came to know God when He saved me. I "experienced" His forgiveness and grace, in Christ.

> **Jeremiah 31:34,** "For they shall all know me, from the least of them unto the greatest of them, saith the Lord: for I will forgive their iniquity, and I will remember their sin no more."

Then, later, under Pastor Pelkey, and by the grace of God, I began to grow in knowledge about Him, and of Him.

When the Lord sent out His disciples and the apostle Paul to spread the gospel, He had them establish other local churches. The New Testament writers often speak of (and directly to) local churches. It is very clear that the Lord wants all believers to be connected to a Biblical local church.

I am glad that I finally did see this truth and did join a scriptural, local, New Testament church. Had I stayed out of church, I know my spiritual growth would have been "stunted" and I would have missed out on all of the blessings the Lord had for me in the fellowship of the local body of believers.

- 8 -

A Message to Seeking Souls

Luke 19:10 *"For the Son of man is come to seek and to save that which was lost."*

The Bible says that there are two groups of people, and every one of us fall into one of those two groups. You are either condemned by our Holy God because of your sin, or you are not condemned because of your faith in Christ and His death on the cross for you, as your substitute.

> **John 3:18,** "He that believeth on him is not condemned: but he that believeth not is condemned already...

Those who are condemned may be very religious, or they may be as worldly as it gets (like I was). God desires that all who are in this group be saved, regardless of their level of religiosity, or lack thereof.

> **2 Peter 3:9,** "The Lord is not slack concerning his promise, as some men count slackness; but is longsuffering to us-ward, not willing that any should perish, but that all should come to repentance."

As I update this chapter of the book, being saved now for over 10 years (2023), I look back on the many new Christians I've met since my own conversion, including my wife, Claudia, who was saved April 12, 2021, and son, Clayton, who was saved days after Claudia.

Claudia, Clayton, and so many others, were saved after intellectually believing the truths of the gospel … attending church … changing many things. It was only after they finally saw and believed in their heart that they were lost, that they went on to be saved. Afterall, if you were never lost, what would you need salvation from?

I believe one of the devil's main strategies is to convince a lost soul that they are not really lost. This must be seen for what it is!

> **Proverbs 14:12,** "There is a way which seemeth right unto a man, but the end thereof are the ways of death."

> **2 Corinthians 13:5,** "Examine yourselves, whether ye be in the faith; prove your own selves. Know ye not your own selves, how that Jesus Christ is in you, except ye be reprobates?"

No one is found who wasn't first lost. When were you lost? If you are not willing to admit that you are lost, then you cannot be saved. But the moment you realize you're a lost sinner, and you need Him more than anything else, He will be there to catch you!

> **Jeremiah 29:13,** "And ye shall seek me, and find me, when ye shall search for me with all your heart."

A lost sinner will naturally pray for salvation, but God's method of saving sinners is by grace, through faith, not by repeating a prayer, getting baptized, or even agreeing with the truth of the gospel intellectually. A decision is the beginning, but faith (resting in Christ and His finished work for you) is what saves. Saving faith is not about doing anything but being in heart-agreement with God about your sin, and *resting* in what Christ has already done for you.

I personally know many Christians, including my own Pastor, who were in church, agreeing with the truth of the Bible for years before they were saved. They had to get over their pride and come to the realization that all they ever really had was religion.

My pastor said it well when he said, "I got 2 Corinthians 5:17 backwards. It says, 'if any man be in Christ, he is a new creature' but I thought, 'if any man be a new creature, he must be in Christ.'"

Turning over a new leaf is not enough. The leaf itself is already dead. You can work at keeping the bad fruit off of a bad tree, but it will always produce bad fruit! The tree must be cut down completely, in order for a new tree to grow in its place and produce good fruit. "You must be born again."

Another strategy of the devil is to convince a lost person that he is saved because he is not like others. I was of this mentality for a while before I finally realized I was lost. I would think to myself, "Everyone is a sinner, and I'm not nearly as bad as many people. God will surely keep me from hell somehow." I failed to realize that the number of condemned people has nothing to do with God's holiness! Whether there is one lost person in the world, or all of mankind were lost, God's holiness does not change. He must punish sin.

Deuteronomy 32:4, "He is the Rock, his work is perfect: for all his ways are judgment: a God of truth and without iniquity, just and right is he."

Romans 3:10, "As it is written, There is none righteous, no, not one . . ."

Romans 6:23, "For the wages of sin is death"

Hebrews 9:27, "And as it is appointed unto men once to die, but after this the judgment . . ."

But when a person "gets lost" (realizes they are lost), as the Lord said to that scribe in Mark 12:34, "Thou art not far from the kingdom of God."

Mark 12:34, "And when Jesus saw that he answered discreetly, he said unto him, Thou art not far from the kingdom of God . . ."

Romans 6:23 goes on to give us the solution:

Romans 6:23, "... but the gift of God is eternal life through Jesus Christ our Lord."

It is in the natural heart of man to believe that we must earn anything that is worth having. In 2 Kings 5 we read of Naaman, the captain of the host of the king of Syria, who was a leper. Naaman was instructed by the prophet to simply wash in the Jordan seven times, and he would be healed of his leprosy. But Naaman rejected this offer.

> **2 Kings 5:11-12,** "But Naaman was wroth, and went away, and said, Behold, I thought, He will surely come out to me, and stand, and call on the name of the Lord his God, and strike his hand over the place, and recover the leper. Are not Abana and Pharpar, rivers of Damascus, better than all the waters of Israel? may I not wash in them, and be clean? So he turned and went away in a rage."

This is why man looks for justification in something they produce.

- Religiosity
- Good works
- Baptism
- Communion
- Comparison to others
- Knowledge
- Theology
- Prayer
- Turning from a sinful lifestyle

The list goes on and on. While these things are good, they do not, in themselves, save. I have heard many others point to what they consider to be miracles in their life as proof of their salvation. This too, is vanity, and not Biblical. Whether they really were miracles or not, God can do miracles in a lost man's life, just as He can a saved man's life.

Only a surrender of self to Christ and His blood atonement on the cross will save.

2 Corinthians 5:21, "For he hath made him to be sin for us, who knew no sin; that we might be made the righteousness of God in him."

Christ died for the ungodly. He died for you. Do you believe God? Then rest in His Son, who invites you to come to Him and receive forgiveness of sin and enjoy eternal life with Him.

John 10:9, "I am the door: by me if any man enter in, he shall be saved, and shall go in and out, and find pasture."

2 Corinthians 9:15, "Thanks be unto God for his unspeakable gift."

John 1:12, "But as many as received him, to them gave he power to become the sons of God, even to them that believe on his name . . ."

Matthew 11:28-30, "Come unto me, all ye that labour and are heavy laden, and I will give you rest.

Take my yoke upon you, and learn of me; for I am meek and lowly in heart: and ye shall find rest unto your souls. For my yoke is easy, and my burden is light."

Matthew 19:25-26, "When his disciples heard it, they were exceedingly amazed, saying, Who then can be saved?

But Jesus beheld them, and said unto them, With men this is impossible; but with God all things are possible."

Matthew 9:10-13, "And it came to pass, as Jesus sat at meat in the house, behold, many publicans and sinners came and sat down with him and his disciples.

And when the Pharisees saw it, they said unto his disciples, Why eateth your Master with publicans and sinners? But when Jesus heard that, he said unto them, They that be whole need not a physician, but they that are sick.

But go ye and learn what that meaneth, I will have mercy, and not sacrifice: for I am not come to call the righteous, but sinners to repentance."

Isaiah 64:6, "But we are all as an unclean thing, and all our righteousnesses are as filthy rags; and we all do fade as a leaf; and our iniquities, like the wind, have taken us away."

Isaiah 55:1, "Ho, every one that thirsteth, come ye to the waters, and he that hath no money; come ye, buy, and eat; yea, come, buy wine and milk without money and without price."

Ephesians 2:8-9, "For by grace are ye saved through faith; and that not of yourselves: it is the gift of God: Not of works, lest any man should boast."

Matthew 11:28-30, "Come unto me, all ye that labour and are heavy laden, and I will give you rest.

Take my yoke upon you, and learn of me; for I am meek and lowly in heart: and ye shall find rest unto your souls.

For my yoke is easy, and my burden is light."

Romans 6:23 "For the wages of sin is death; but the gift of God is eternal life through Jesus Christ our Lord."

Isaiah 53, "5 But he was wounded for our transgressions, he was bruised for our iniquities ... with his stripes we are healed.

6 All we like sheep have gone astray; we have turned every one to his own way; and the Lord hath laid on him the iniquity of us all.

...

10 Yet it pleased the Lord to bruise him; he hath put him to grief: when thou shalt make his soul an offering for sin,

...

11 He [the Father] shall see of the travail of his [the Son's] soul, and shall be satisfied: by his knowledge shall my righteous servant justify many; for he shall bear their iniquities.

12 [He] made intercession for the transgressors."

- 9 -

The Importance of Assurance

2 Corinthians 13:5 *"Examine yourselves, whether ye be in the faith; prove your own selves. Know ye not your own selves, how that Jesus Christ is in you, except ye be reprobates?"*

I f you were to pick up a modern-day Christian children's book, chances are, this would be the overall message that you would read: "You were created by God. God is good. Jesus loves us and died for our sin so that we can be saved. We should live for Him since he died for us, by helping other people and doing good."

This message is true. However, there is a grave error in it. The error is in the exclusion of the necessity of conversion!

Children born into many American homes today are told from the moment they exit the womb that they are good with God because of Jesus' death on the cross. They never hear the words our Lord spoke to Nicodemus:

John 3:3, "Verily, verily, I say unto thee, Except a man be born again, he cannot see the kingdom of God.."

Is it any wonder then that most professed Christians couldn't tell you the day they became a Christian? Most will tell you the day they were baptized, or the day they said the "sinner's prayer," or they'll just say, "for as long as I remember."

We cannot rest our soul's eternity on a prayer someone told us to pray before they told us we were saved. Only God can tell a person they are truly saved, and that is through Biblical conversion, which is the result of a resting, saving faith in Christ alone. We must always go by the Bible, not what we think or what someone else tells us.

> **Proverbs 14:12,** "There is a way which seemeth right unto a man, but the end thereof are the ways of death."

The Bible says we must be born again. It says that the Holy Spirit comes to abide in the heart of all believers.

> **Romans 8:9,** "But ye are not in the flesh, but in the Spirit, if so be that the Spirit of God dwell in you. Now if any man have not the Spirit of Christ, he is none of his.

It tells us that many will come to Him, as false converts, trying to convince Him that they really were saved. These are professing Christians (they call Him "Lord") but were never born again.

> **Matthew 7:22-24,** "Many will say to me in that day, Lord, Lord, have we not prophesied in thy name? . . . and in thy name done many wonderful works? And then will I profess unto them, I never knew you: depart from me, ye that work iniquity."

In the Apostle Paul's letter to the Thessalonians, Paul states that he knows the election of the believers he speaks to because they received the gospel, not in word only, but in *power*, and in the Holy Ghost, and in *much assurance and joy*. He goes on to state that they didn't just have a moment, but they continued on. They were followers of the Lord during great persecution, when compromise would save them a lot of pain. Yet, they didn't compromise.

> **1 Thessalonians 1:4-6,** "Knowing, brethren beloved, your election of God. For our gospel came not unto you in word only, but also in power, and in the Holy Ghost, and in much assurance; as ye know what manner of men we were among you for your sake. And ye became followers of us, and of the Lord, having received the word in much affliction, with joy of the Holy Ghost."

Paul, speaking to the believers in the church at Corinth, said that receiving the Holy Spirit is our "earnest" and "seal."

> **2 Corinthians 1:20-22,** "Now he which stablisheth us with you in Christ, and hath anointed us, is God; who hath also sealed us, and given the earnest of the Spirit in our hearts.."

Again, in his letter to the believers in the church at Ephesus, Paul says the Holy Spirit is our "earnest" and "seal."

> **Ephesians 1:13-14,** "In whom ye also trusted, after that ye heard the word of truth, the gospel of your salvation: in whom also after that ye believed, ye were sealed with that holy Spirit of promise, which is the earnest of our inheritance until the redemption of the purchased possession, unto the praise of his glory."

An earnest is a deposit made in order to confirm intent to complete a transaction. When an offer is accepted on a home, the seller receives "earnest money." That is money given by the buyer to show the seller that they have made up their mind and the full transition will happen soon.

If the seller wasn't sure whether they received the earnest or not, that earnest money would do them no good.

A seal is defined as, "concluding, establishing, or securing (something) definitely, excluding the possibility of reversal or loss."

Paul was not speaking of a "maybe/maybe not" salvation. He wasn't speaking of an unknown salvation. He was speaking of a *sure* and *secure* salvation *that you know about*.

In his letter to the Romans, Paul says the Spirit "bears witness," or reveals to us, that we are the children of God.

> **Romans 8:16,** "The Spirit itself beareth witness with our spirit, that we are the children of God."

In the book of Acts Luke records the words of Peter as he addresses some Pharisees. Peter speaks of the witness of the Spirit as well. He doesn't leave room for the interpretation that only some believers have the witness of the

Spirit. He speaks as though all true believers have this witness.

> **Acts 15:8**, "And God, which knoweth the hearts, bare them witness, giving them the Holy Ghost, even as he did unto us."

Although we do see a past, present, and future tense of the word, "saved" used in the Scripture (saved from the penalty, power, and presence), we do not find in the Bible a progressive salvation. We do not see any examples of people who were "kind of saved" and then "mostly saved" and then "finally saved." We see a very definitive salvation that happens at a point in time, just as Paul's conversion on the road to Damascus. We see people who either are saved or are not saved -- nothing in between.

We do not see any form of prayer as the basis for salvation in the Word of God either. I am convinced that some do get saved saying the "sinners prayer." However, as Paul Washer once said, "they were saved in spite of the sinner's prayer, not because of it." They were saved because at some point during that prayer (or maybe even in the aisle on the way to the alter) they gave up on themselves and trusted in Jesus Christ as their savior.

Many Christians, including many great reformers and preachers, have salvation testimonies published online and freely available. They speak of a point in time when they knew their sin was forgiven — when they were born again. Three things are always the same: the instantaneous peace that comes into the heart, the knowledge of the forgiveness of sin, and a progressive change afterward.

Charles Wesley said it well in an early hymn that he wrote:

> "Long my imprisoned spirit lay; Fast bound in sin and nature's night; Thine eye diffused a quickening ray, I woke, the dungeon flamed with light; My chains fell off, my heart was free, I rose, went forth, and followed thee."

His brother, John, described the moment when he was saved with these words:

> "Someone read from Luther's Preface to the Epistle to Romans. About 8:45 p.m. while he was describing the change which God works in the heart through faith in Christ, I felt my heart strangely warmed. I felt I did trust in Christ, Christ alone for salvation; and an assurance was given me that He had taken away my sins, even mine, and saved me from the law of sin and death."
>
> Taken from *The Journal of John Wesley* (Public Domain)

Charles H. Spurgeon, "The Prince of Preachers," described his moment of salvation like this:

> "That happy day, when I found the Saviour . . . I could have leaped, I could have danced; there was no expression, however fanatical, which would have been out of keeping with the joy of my spirit at that hour . . .
>
> I thought I could have sprung from the seat on which I sat, and have called out . . . "I am forgiven! I am forgiven! A monument of grace! A sinner saved by blood!"
>
> Taken from *C.H. Spurgeon's Autobiography* (Public Domain)

The words of the famous song "Amazing Grace" by John Newton describe the moment when he was saved by grace:

> Amazing grace, How sweet the sound
> That saved a wretch like me.
> I once was lost, but now am found,
> Was blind, but now I see.
>
> 'Twas grace that taught my heart to fear,
> And grace my fears relieved.
> How precious did that grace appear
> The hour I first believed.

The words of the popular modern song "He Touched Me" written by Bill Gaither describe this moment of salvation as well:

> Shackled by a heavy burden
> 'Neath a load of guilt and shame
> Then the hand of Jesus touched me
> And now I am no longer the same
> He touched me, Oh, He touched me
> And Oh the joy that floods my soul
> Something happened and now I know
> He touched me and made me whole

I heard this song for the first time in church, nine months or so after the Lord saved me. The first time I heard it I rejoiced because that is exactly how I had been describing the moment when I was born again to people. "It was like God touched me! Joy flooded my soul, and I was no longer the same!"

Since then, I have heard the testimonies of many others who gave the same witness. All of these people had a moment when peace came into their hearts, their sin burden was gone, and an incredible internal change began. *It was real!*

Hearing that there is such a reality to saving faith, many who do not have the same assurance accuse those of us who proclaim this Biblical doctrine as being, "charismatic." This is not true. We only proclaim the truth that *there is a reality to saving faith and a reality to walking in the presence of the Lord.*

Others claim that it is judgmental to proclaim these truths. Yet the Lord Himself, as well as several writers of the Scriptures, clearly proclaimed them.

> **John 3:3,** "Jesus answered and said unto him, Verily, verily, I say unto thee, Except a man be born again, he cannot see the kingdom of God."

Suppose you were watching a man walk toward a cliff. He told you that he had a parachute and that he was fine, but he couldn't show you his parachute. Would you say, "Okay, great!" and leave him alone? If you could, I would question your love for that person. No, you would plead with him to *make sure* if you cared at all for him. That is not being judgmental, that is loving that person.

Before the Lord saved me on that cold December afternoon, I didn't know there was a reality to salvation. I didn't know when you are born again, you know it. I had not been brought up in a church where people talk about "being saved." Although in the past I had apparently heard at least one real salvation testimony (before Pastor Morrow went on to be with the Lord, he reminded me that he had told me his salvation testimony when we first met), the reality of saving faith was not something I was looking for. I just knew I had a sin problem and needed forgiveness. I just knew that I fell short. I just knew that there was something more and intellectual ascent to some belief system would not fill that void. I needed the Way, the Truth, and the Life, and nothing else would do!

I came to this reality/experience before I ever read or heard of the experiences of others. I wasn't even aware the Bible taught so much about *real* salvation.

I had a real experience with God that evening, and He has thoroughly changed me from the inside out. I am a new person with a new heart and new desires. I have a burden for lost souls, and I can truly say that I love the Lord Jesus Christ and His law.

There truly is a reality to saving faith. If you haven't experienced this reality, will you come to the Lord Jesus right now as a helpless, condemned sinner who desperately needs a Savior? Come now. Tomorrow may never come!

Is there anything more serious than this? Get into His Word. Run to the cross. Cry out to Him like blind Bartemaeus. Repent and *believe the Gospel*. Do you believe God's Word?

> **Matthew 11:28-30,** "Come unto me, all ye that labour and are heavy laden, and I will give you rest. Take my yoke upon you, and learn of me; for I am meek and lowly in heart: and ye shall find rest unto your souls. For my yoke is easy, and my burden is light."

> **Mark 10:47-48,** "And when he heard that it was Jesus of Nazareth, he began to cry out, and say, Jesus, thou son of David, have mercy on me.

And many charged him that he should hold his peace: but he cried the more a great deal, Thou son of David, have mercy on me."

Revelation 22:17, "And the Spirit and the bride say, Come. And let him that heareth say, Come. And let him that is athirst come. And whosoever will, let him take the water of life freely."

John 6:37, "Him that cometh to me I will in no wise cast out."

Contact the author personally:
Email: contact@EternalAnswers.org
Phone: (812) 698-7659 (call or text)

Other Resources

Read the Bible online for free at:
BibleGateway.com

If you would like to hear more from the author, videos
are available at: Facebook.com/EternalAnswers.

Find answers to commonly asked questions about God,
the Bible, this life, and the life to come, straight from the
Bible, on our ministry website at:
EternalAnswers.org

Read, *"What Does God Want From Me?"* a short booklet
which presents the gospel, and a shorter version of my
own salvation testimony, in PDF format at:
TheRealityOfSavingFaith.com/booklet

Watch salvation testimony videos at:
TheRealityOfSavingFaith.com/saved

www.ingramcontent.com/pod-product-compliance
Lightning Source LLC
Chambersburg PA
CBHW020509030426
42337CB00011B/306